A Fervour of Truth

CHRONICLING THE LIFE OF A POET

Lindsay Sawyer

authorHOUSE®

AuthorHouse™
1663 Liberty Drive
Bloomington, IN 47403
www.authorhouse.com
Phone: 1-800-839-8640

Published by AuthorHouse   01/14/2013

ISBN: 978-1-4817-0915-6 (sc)
ISBN: 978-1-4772-5812-5 (e)

Library of Congress Control Number: 2012915420

Contents

Part 4
Citations of Life

Part 5
Zeal, In Favour of Devotion

Part 1

Youthful
Household

Writer

She creates history.

With every word written, on that

Infamous sheet of lined paper.

An escape from

The realities of the world.

Desperately clinging, to the hope

That trust will lead us in the right direction

Insignificance creates . . .

Anything at all.

And the sentences she scrolls

Will be the beginnings,

Of a life forever dreamt

In that mystical time

Where fantasies meet sleep.

Light

This is a tale about a man, and darling daughter too.

At first sight, his love beamed bright

As daddies always do.

This baby was his light in life, pristine perfection without price.

He vowed to do all he could

Working hard was understood,

Labour was his living, perpetually with his goal in view.

He was gone, for many a year building up his earned career,

While dreaming of his lovely light.

As time grew older, as did she; his lovely light was now a teen.

Upon returning home one day

He learned his girl had gone away.

Days on end, he tried to find, the daughter who had left him cry.

When finally, he spoke to her

There was no instance to concur.

Watching Father walk away, she thought of him in prior days;

Dad who liked to run and play,

Dad who helped her in dismay.

Will she ever know that man? Will this be the reprimand?

That shatters every memory,

Or is this only daunting dreams?

Days then quickly turned to years, never speaking without tears

Of the one light, longed to glimpse

With hugs and love and happiness.

Eventually, the occasion came, to speak on terms un-bluntly

Leaving out the hard, the sad

Devices for an easy fate, not so true, and very late.

But then a miracle as they say; a little boy came their way.

That lovely light, gave birth to

An infant lad; to start anew.

The prospect that once bound them, at last established once again.

They talked, they shared of days long missed

While baby slept in their midst.

Comrade

A comrade whose alliance has
Served me through my years.
The one in which knows my life
Of laughter and of tears.

A comrade whose young memories
Are much the same as mine.
And always stood beside me
Throughout the tests of time.

This comrade could find faults
Of mine, and tell me in a whim,
Sore feelings would be shared at times
After that, accepting them.

A comrade who works hard
Deserving all he takes,
This comrade finds his way in life
Despite the trialed stakes.

Comrade I have learnt from you,
As I hope that you can see
Thank you to our parents
Who brought you here to me.

Mama: A Commencement

Mama, Mama, hear me please,

Our disposition, one.

We met from times before you knew

Inhibitions; there were none.

You nurtured me in times of sorrow

And provided times of joy,

You taught me ways of fancy free

Inventions to deploy!

There were although, grief filled moments

In my juvenile method

We could not find a happy place,

The illusion justly boded.

Fighting feuds became the norm
We could not co-exist
Losing faith in later days,
Our friendship is released.

I think of all the years we lost
To mournful, forlorn fights,
Would it ever be the same?
I'd think with solemn spite.

Night-time stories

Tonight I hear sorrowed cries.

Accompanied by lonely lies.

Dusk falls fast

With nightly sighs,

Giving rest to weary eyes.

The Pen has Writ

If I can't expect perfection,

Out of every single action

And, immaculate satisfaction

In an extreme hypnotic fashion

Then I will have to go and ration

Every kind Of Passion!

Pride

Forever inept in humanity's mysteries,
Memories made
Sealed in history.

Take life fast, or take it slow
Become a believer,
In human soul.

Know that now
In this time, we are here
To always thrive.

Enjoy the moment

Live out loud

Dare your dreams

Speak out, be proud!

Do You Hear Me?

So many thoughts lost in oblivion
Ending in regret, dismissal, contempt.
I want to speak out and be heard
Do you hear me?

You will share with me,
Your greatest fears
Your most difficult trials,
Do you hear me?

We will converse,
Continuing on, pretending to understand
This thing we call 'being'
But do you hear me?

You may live to strive

I will love to thrive

To live in a world

With so much chaos;

To conquer our greatest conquest, Do you hear me?

Verdict

So many hours wasted

In the dim of hazy desire.

Life generates

A certain multitude of havoc.

Wouldn't you enjoy to

Escape?

An elusive dream,

Hiding the obvious idiosyncrasies of life

Sitting here, in solitary detention

Gives me impending insight

For days to pursue.

The Voyage

Adventure;

For anyone who seeks more,

Than the mundane existence

We strive so hard to maintain.

Part 2

Accounts of the Down and Out

The Truth of Desperation

Forged, was the love which I foolishly bought into.

Secrets of history, continuously spinning.

Never to be made known.

Forged, was the hope that I desperately gripped,

With hands that bled from a

lover's libel.

Forged, was the reality

Which I saw through eyes of dappled envy.

Hues of sober gray.

Forged, was the life I seemingly loved.

Hopes of fantasies that never came to pass.

Realities of truthful desperation.

Shame

You write this word of shame to her, one too many times.

How many days, did you spend

Looming over lines?

You need not know her story, assumptions always lead.

You've showed your skilful hand.

Has the devil paid his deed?

How many times before have you, lashed out in ruined ways?

I think of all the saddened souls

You've hurt so much today.

She will never know your goal, or the life in which you lay

She will, although find comfort in

The knowledge of your shame.

The Liaison

Some days I wish that fatal night
Of interrupted disposition,
Was just a fleeting memory
And our moves could be forgiven.

For every time a place like this
Resides within my heart
The manner which we both may share
Will soon begin to part.

Lust can be forgiven,
Love can be beseeching
And somewhere in between
Is where I find us seeking.

Will you ever follow through
And make this something right?
Or is it destined for certain loss
A lifetime lived on mights?

For once I wish that fate
Would lead me where to go
So I could believe in you
To seize this current ride.

Aftermath

This morning is unforgiving

Regarding thoughts of life.

Conflict, bounds to every corner

And an envious miasma, is all that's visible.

I only wish that clarity, would once more

Grace my mind,

Allowing me to take control of this life of mine.

Possibilities fill tomorrow's air,

Just far enough away, to know

Time is of an essential factor.

An Ill-fated Apathy

Distant memories; fading rapid,
Of lovers come then vanished
Thoughts of points in the past
Which now just feel mistaken.

Feelings though, may approach then go
And with this we must find;
Our hardships in the past endured,
Without them pressing on.

I feel uneasy, cannot quite speak
Of trials from before
You see the word, indifference
Has me truly frightened more.

So many sore words said

Without them we'd be fine

To do this all again

Would be a lapse in time.

Thoughts

Reverie, or memory?

Or is it just alike?

I think of you,

In days of now, and regrettably

Rejoice.

Subsistence seen through

Seminal times, yet

Still regress to lesser rhymes!

Motives which had caused our part,

Only now a reminiscence.

Deceitful visions, chilling dreams

Soaring through my essence.

An added point of bliss,

Investments of favoured fortune,

Charming tricks, illuminated, all that is magnificent;

Perhaps the imaginings that I speak of.

Detached, is one life lived

Amidst bust and hopeless times,

Still I see your ominous eyes

Reminding me of longing.

Temporary Title

A funny little thing called love
Had snuck into these lines.
But quickly finding out of it,
I tossed it to the nines!

What a pity
It would have been,
To endure a reading through
Lovey dovey, disgusting things
I wouldn't have a clue!

If only life could be like this
With an eraser to remove
Those nauseating moments when
No memories can sooth.

The Bereft Inn

My heart is heavy, my will be free
Never again will they see.
I'll give my soul to know one
It is mine to keep
I cannot go on, searching for outs
Of inns that house the meek.

Leaning on no one I will
Thrive on,
Until my last mourning's dawn.
I see myself as jaded
For this I will not trust
A touch which says
He loves me
Believing turns to rust.

I find myself avenging

A distant disbelief

maybe one day

When all has cleared

I'll understand

This lodge of fear.

Evolution

My mind races, with lessons learned

What do they mean, when did I turn, into this being

Of right and wrong, can't we all just

Play along?

I long to be me once more, again I want to fearlessly soar.

Yet now there is a drifting air,

Not to argue

I would not dare.

Never again, will I see a colour for its marvelous rays

A shadow for its mysterious haze, this is a trade-off we all must
face,

To gain the knowledge

Is to lose your pace.

Verbal Veracity

The city sleeps with solitude.

As daybreak moves stealthily

To fruition,

Contemplation of undertakings

In the previous hours of obscurity

Weigh too heavily

On my feeble frame.

All that some may see

Mundane,

Materialize.

I think of

You,

And know this can never be.

Part 3

Issue of Angst

With Child

A strange and rapid feeling, wells within my wits
The thought of Motherhood; stabbing, sudden, swift.
For all to see I'm barefoot, eighteen years old, yet young.

How can I raise a child? A nauseating thought,
My world has turned askew, with unforgiving fraught.
There it is again! That sickening, horrid ache.

Could it be this child? The reflection makes me quake.
A living human being, residing in my womb
If cherished and beloved, allowing it to bloom.

This is a thought, unsought, until this recent mark
A pronouncement of existence, not a lowly lark.
I stumble on this sentiment, still barbed to the stroke.

Could I be a Mother? Its prospect, quite intriguing.

At times it will be painful and rather troublesome

Yet could it be all worth it, to try to rise above?

A child, to teach, a child to esteem

A child which I'd watch establish,

A child, primed from me.

A strange and sudden feeling wells within my brain

I am going to be a Mother, I crave I cannot feign.

A Child of Dreams

The child which I longed to see, now was fading in front
Of me.

How could I halt this tormented pain, how could I pause this current
Game?

A wretched feeling deep inside

Knowing that she won't abide.

Six long months I knew her for, if only I could have three more.

Anger strikes with assault

Faith is futile with this result.

I briefly think of days to come, and realize I will not be, 'Mom'.

Her eyes will never see the light, her face will never smile bright.

To think of her upon my breast

Creates a world of unjust stress.

Then as quickly as it started,
She and I had fully parted.

Tears begin to shed down me
For the child which I longed to see.

The Mechanism

Tap. Tap. Tap.

Sounds of my soon ill-fitted fortune.

An intervening contraption

To *halt*

My life as I know it.

Discreet basis reminds me

Of better days.

Find solace modest one.

Mama: Closing Moments

Mama, Mama hear me please

Devastation's struck.

I need you more than ever now

As I cry from painful destiny.

In recent days, I thought I'd know

A daughter's love in which,

Would fill me with a bond in time

So intimate and prosperous.

My babe is faltering

With a diligence that's fierce.

And will depart, but leave behind

A heart so very pierced.

I now know, how you felt
Desertions desolate
To have you hold me at this time
A dream I can't forget.

Mama, Mama, thank you so
You stood beside me when
All was lost in worlds undue
And prayed with me, Amen.

Paradoxical Nightmares

Last night I held you.

I kissed your temple, so soft, so sweet.

Your smell enveloped me

In perplexed sorrow.

To part in such a way; overwhelming.

Your sounds of life brought

Life back to me.

Your hushed cooing

Allowed serenity to reside simply this night.

To part in such a way; helpless.

Once waking,

I found only a lovely recollection

Was left behind.

To part in such a way; haunting.

My Sickness

Your make-believe image endures my roving mind, and I cannot get
Rid of it

Although I truly try.

So I will turn to poorly drink to run you out of sight

And the ones who call me friend

Will pour

To strengthen fight. I do not have the force

To do this on my own

How else expel this memory I intake every night?

Please excuse my sickness

For I am not all well

My plea is to be free of recall

Which I'm sure I never will.

For days and days, I will try

To purge you once again, I cannot receive the rest I need

To halt this harsh transgression.

Please oh please, what can I do?

Give me subtle hints.

And once again, the ones who I call friend,

Will pour,

To strengthen fight.

Please excuse my sickness

For I am not all well

My plea is to be free of recall

Which I'm sure I never will.

I drown myself into, an existence that is strictly perilous
Still in darkness the nightmares come of you and reminiscence.
During day, it's easier to hide my sorrowing angst
Laughing, playing, working hard
To portray I am, 'survivor'.
Will I take this poison, down into my core
To wipe away, the blatant pain
Which I can't ignore?

Please excuse my sickness
For I am not all well
My plea is to be free of recall
Which I know I never will.

Days Past

I take leaps and strides
Relief is a word
I've long since forgotten.
I sigh, while the shriek
Of days past
Floods motionless
Through my veins.
The fear is gone,
But leaves behind
The ageless stench
Of dismal cries.

Ode to An Angel

Loss is our last misery,

If only you'd wake up and see.

The clouds have lifted,

The storm abroad, and new beginnings

Start from sod.

The past a beautiful memory,

But in the past you're meant to be.

If only you'd wake up and see.

I catch your sense from time to time,

I only wonder if you find mine.

I know that life may take sharp turns,

Look to your soul

Find what's learned.

One day is greater than a thousand years

Of heartache, hurt and painful tears.

I can now finally see

You have justly been set free,

To live a life less recently

Happy, joyful, as can be.

If only you'd wake up and see.

Solitude.

My body exudes,

A sigh of relief

As I finally, am given the

Allowance

Of the outpouring emotion that,

Embodies me.

I take no lament

Of days past.

Yet a forward motion is,

Seized.

Action, something longed for

In days to follow.

Being here

In this place in the world;

Life will lead me

Where I need to

Go.

Ivory Sky

Familiar sounds,
Evidence of a lifetime lost.
How many moments pass
Never to be thought of in
Later days?

A peculiar feeling
Enthralls my mind
This early morn,
Notes made yesterday
Take no toll, on today's Ivory Sky.

And the light of tomorrow

Shall not reign clear

Until that exact space in time

When we can be given new eyes

Once more.

Part 4

Citations
of Life

A Place in Time

It was a vast time on this place we call earth.

We could fall into the depths of imagination

And become a buoyant force,

Anything at all.

The sounds of beings intermingling as one,

And the dire noises would drift off

As though never there at all.

No one could recognize rhyme nor reason,

Chaos belonging to every corner,

Yet not scathing a single soul.

The bodies in the room became benevolent

At that moment in time

Dreams were real,

Just close enough to reach out and touch

Then flitting off into the sudden distance . . .

Midnight Records

The sound of screeching tires at midnight
Enchants my ears.
Suddenly I have an unattainable urge
To write these words down.

So many countless hours pondering;
Survival/worship/cupidity
And all that is in between
Saddles my common sense.

It is as though
A flabbergasted mimic, has entered me
And sentences alone
Cannot explain the feelings I grasp.

If a writer's greatest fear

Is to be short of tongue,

Why does stillness

Comfort so?

Frost befalls

The boulevard meandering,

The path ambiguous, silver trees skip to sounds

Of cricking in the wintriness.

Soft and subtle memoirs, flood

In like a temptress

Of days stretched passed,

Yet oh so stuck, in my reminiscence.

A solitary creature,

Shifts lightly through my vision

Sufficiency leading to

. . . Infringement of my thoughts

Potentially,

In future days

Forgiveness will be given.

Viewpoint Juncture

My tea and I sit sombrely atop

This city roof, and gaze upon metropolis

Feeling quite remote.

The merchants down below

Set up their booths

While a drifter passes by,

And the businessmen dressed

Smart in suit, are

Running for the transit line.

Children skip down the street

Whilst asking mothers 'why?'

My screening time is shattered

By the noise of lively breathing

That floods quickly into range,

Memories of times well shared

(Compassion somehow changed.)

Connections linked from down below

To that eventful street so modest,

Rapport is felt to strangers,

Those I'll never meet.

Trees of jade, skew tenderly

Amongst the urban air,

Resulting in a complex

Of cities to compare.

Attitude

Serenity, peace, an undying faith

Among life and its hectic ways.

Allowing yourself to forget,

For moments even seconds

All the battles that face the future.

The ability to bask in solitude

Creating creativity

Pushing aside the negative

Pulling positivity close enough

To reach out and grasp the greatness of anything.

Surf

The water brigades into these unyielding rocks,

With no uncertainty guiding its way.

Anecdotes told from long ago,

Vanished in a mass of havoc waste.

Unearthed judgment,

A sad and threatening place.

Pallid surfers find sanctuary

Atop their haven bed.

Only to take rest,

When the gusts of heaven settle.

Robbing respite;

Redundant luxuries.

Alas, the breeze exchange!

Verse of the Indisposed

Life has gone astray, favours with a price tag.

I am the eyes that hold your stare

That unforgiving truth,

You'll pass me by and watch me cry,

A tear for spiteful couth.

Will you ever think of me while lounging in your suite?

Of jewels, wealth and luxury

As I quiver on the street.

You will say, it's no fault but my own

That I live in ruined ways

What will become of the kids, I cannot feed today?

They'll grow older knowing

This is the only way.

An empty hand remains, a beggar's means for gain

I will not ever stop

Despite this stabbing pain.

After all, 'tis all I know and habits hard to break

If only there was hope, I'd see for heaven's sakes.

Onlooker

I take a look at the surrounding humans who fill the seats on this
City transit bus.

I ponder the thought on mankind, yet it quickly fades away . . .

A snide comment is hurtled my way, rebutted with a forced glare I
Turn my glance to another.

(If it weren't for these damned untamed egos, maybe the thought of
Peace on earth wouldn't be such a joke.)

A man dressed for business sits three seats ahead,

Listening to headphones he gives no acknowledgment to another
Breathing being on this bus.

Soon after noticing this man

His counter opposite appears,

A frail woman,

Dressed in torn attire and smelling of stale cigarettes.

Unlike the man to whom no other paid attention,

The entirety of the bus looks up when the woman appears

If only for paying her fare in dimes and nickels,

Regardless.

As she makes her way down the aisle she passes empty seats,

Goes directly for the man dressed for business.

He takes a quick look as if to say,

'Really?'

Then shuffles over to allow her to sit.

She gives him a friendly smile

He turns his head to the window and gazes idly by.

Have inhibitions and self-righteousness

Become so overbearing in today's world, is it too much to ask to return a gracious gesture?

I hear a ding

And the man removes himself from his awkward situation.

I guess this is how life goes,

If the string is strung, there will always be a time and place to pull.

"Jump!"

"Dive in, jump in, that water is grand!"

I wailed to my dread-filled friends!

The jellyfish swam round the loop of the

Pool

Performing as though it was home.

The water was cold, chilling me

Full to the bone

Yet fulfilling my every urge

My teeth were a chatter,

My knees clicked and clacked

However the water kept calling me home.

I swam in that water for forty-five plus

Pretending it was not a bother.

And when I emerged

My body was bitter, from indulging in such

Predisposed peril.

It never occurred, I was being absurd

And acting for something not said.

From the point which I leaped, not another would dare

And they stared with uncomfortable eyes

I continued to hurdle over that hang

Until drowning my lies were declined.

Once More

Naive was I when we walked,

That significant summer's eve.

I silently begged it to be, that you would be,

Perfectly gentlemanly.

The sea swam up to that rock-strewn ledge,

Where we sat, beside one another.

We shared our stories, tales and more

As well as a deep notion thought.

Yet as fine as it was, and as sharp as it was

I now feel a great remorse.

For an absence at hand

On the part of me, as I daydreamed of another.

Thought I could put him aside in my mind
Unfortunately this was not so.
I left you alone and I went home
To trifle through papers, (scrap and attached to bindings)

To find a clue, of a number or two
In direction of where he could be.
Ultimately, I forgot you with ease
And moved onward with, another.

I think of you now,
Hoping of no ill judgment
For when I left you alone
On that rock-strewn ledge
It was quite ungentlemanly.

Part 5

Zeal, In Favour of Devotion

My Mind

We live mutually,
What they call mankind.
No one knows the pain
Which continues in our mind.

We put on those candid smiles,
Pretend to live our life.
No one knows the pain
Which continues in our mind.

I see you, and you see me
Suddenly we can't agree, what fate's to be,
No one knows the pain
Which continues in our mind.

You make outrageous comments,
Pertaining to our life,
You can't control every move
You simply cannot strive.

So in the end, my long lost friend
My lasting words are this,
What we had, has gone amiss
It is something you must find.

For no one knows the pain
Which continues in my mind.

A Best Friend's Dream

On an odd and eerie

Urban night

A notion came to me;

Revelations from the past

Reviewed, relieving me to sigh.

He sauntered back into my life

From heartaches hanging on

We chattered of, days long missed

And found the past,

The past.

The void was gone

That caused our part, the first

And fatal time. No more tears

Or vacant struggles,

No more lonely nights.

Laughing love, was

The vision, that never came to be.

Until this odd and eerie eve,

A nighttime filled of

Dreams.

Secrets

Tell me how you feel.

Present to me

Words in which

Only lovers can exchange.

Be true to your feelings,

Thoughts,

Whatever may come.

Cherish me

As no one ever has.

The Feat

The throb of passion, encumbers their bones

Erotic smells.

Timeless moans.

Holding true to the notion, life is fast, enjoys its motion.

An intensified knowledge

Of what's within

Becomes more evident

With every sin.

The feverish sweat

Of craze unfolds

Moves are made . . .

Unwise, yet bold

Upping the stakes,
The heart rate pounds
For the future,
Of its ending rounds.

A peak in which they
both may share
Indescribable manner
Unspeakable air

They sleep.

Alone

It's funny how some women long, for silly little words in song.

Countless years, spent at a distance
Believing, dreaming of your touch
Stewing over moments made
Knowing it can't be the same.

Then again how long can we,
Hide from this true misery?
Today it's just fun and games
Tomorrow who will be to blame?

It's funny how some women long, for silly little words in song.

Will we continue on again
Pretending we are just good friends?
A phenomenon has grazed our path
We were given a second chance.

After all the things we've said
Can we try to make amends?
Will it always be the same?
Simply kissing in the rain.

It's funny how some women long, for silly little words in song.

I for one, would like to be
The woman who you choose to see
And yet I still am at a loss
For what you feel, and at what cost.

Gentleman

Gentle man, oh gentle man

While rootless athwart my

Stirring life, never thought I

Would find,

A pair who could be

Perfectly, fitted

As you and I.

Years that I roamed,

Round the rock of

This globe

I'd think of your

Beautiful face

Imminently, I'd

Implore it to be

You, that I'd somewhere

Find.

Son

Little boy, you came to me in thoughts so far away
A finding in this life could be, so unexpectedly.
Revel in your innocence, so lovely to the touch
Sending thanks to all above, and merit where it's due.
Just when life had got away
Everything was lost,
Forgetting every minute, in moments long forgot.
Frenzy failed as theory, as many can assure
Everlasting faith renewed, from then and now with you.
Reveal your worldly secrets, of how you came to be
Saving me from heartache, so inexplicitly!
Oh my small and handsome boy, expectations beat,
Now we can rejoice in your, utmost entity.

Successor

Her almond eyes captivated

My every ounce of mind

Stillness sitting all around, her and I alone.

Pain within my body, overly accepting it

Merely to entrance in our only time unaided.

She's powerless to speak or move, for her body is not brawny.

I know what she expected

With tiny hands, unyielding.

Her face an instance, among exquisiteness

With wholesomeness and truth.

Then by words so softly spoken

That only we could know

She looked upon me, through almond eyes

With an adoring ambiance.

Time stood tranquil,

For that second, then briskly

Came to pass

A love I only knew in thought

Was finally in my grasp.

The Children We Love

A token of us

The growing babes of our lust

Love, the seed to grow.

The Author's Faith

A steady hand brings trust to this sheet.

A clear mind provides truth, to the words that I write.

Faith and understanding supply the tools of forgiveness

With regards to every scratch and scribble on these haggard lines.

Ingredients to have the world at my fingertips.

As I sit upon this rock, I realize

Everything is up to me!